Five Simple Steps to Improve Your Website's Search Engine Ranking

Five Simple Steps to Improve Your Website's Search Engine Ranking

Effective Search Engine Optimization for Everyone

Pat Bensky

Tracker Press

First Edition
Published in Great Britain 2007
by
Tracker Press

ISBN 0-9546105-3-9

www.trackerpress.com

Contents

Introduction

If your web site doesn't appear in the first few pages of search engine results, people are unlikely to find it. This book shows you how you can easily improve your web site's rankings and get it to regularly make it into the first few pages.

Search Engine Optimization (SEO)

That's what we're talking about: optimizing your web site so that search engines will like it and place it near the top in their search results!

The people who run Internet search engine sites such as Google, MSN, AOL Search, Lycos, and so on, are clever folks who want to provide the best service they can; they want people using their sites to find exactly what they are looking for, quickly and easily. These people don't want to see pages and pages of listings of web sites that don't contain relevant information. So the search engine developers employ all sorts of methods for weeding out irrelevant or inappropriate sites, and ensuring that the most relevant results appear first. Read on and I'll tell you how you can make sure that your web site meets the criteria that will please the search engines and get them to list YOUR site in a prominent position!

"But I'm not a Web Site Designer!"

You don't need to be. You just need to have a web page design program such as Dreamweaver (or one of the less expensive options) and some basic skills.

This method is extremely effective

There are lots of big heavy books that go into all kinds of technical details about search engine optimization. I've boiled it all down into FIVE SIMPLE STEPS that anybody can follow. I can't guarantee that your site will immediately start to come out on top, but I can promise you that you will quickly see a major improvement in your rankings if you follow the five steps. I've seen results happen as quickly as THE FOLLOWING DAY after implementing the procedures described in this book! But let's be realistic - it's more likely to take a couple of weeks for an established site; longer for a brand new one.

Let's get on with it then!

I'm not going to waste your time with a long preamble about theory and why certain things do or do not work – who cares? You just want RESULTS and you want them NOW!

So let's get on with it ...

P.S. I would love to hear any feedback from you - comments, suggestions, success stories, whatever! Please email your comments to
fivesteps@trackerpress.com

About the Author

My name is Pat Bensky. I'm a business owner and author. I don't claim to be an SEO expert; what I DO claim is that I've been using the internet since the very earliest days and have been running websites for my businesses since about 1992. I've spent many hours researching search engine optimization and experimenting with ideas on my web sites, and have boiled it all down to the five simple, effective steps that I describe in this book. You'll find the book enjoyable to read and very informative.

– Pat Bensky

Step One: Send in the Robots!

Robots, spiders, web crawlers ... they are known by various names. Their job is to roam around the Internet gathering information about web sites. The information they gather can be used for various purposes, such as indexing web pages for search engines — which is the thing that most interests us.

Of course, these kinds of robot are not made of metal and positronic brains; they are just computer programs.

All the search engines use robots to gather information about pages on the Web and index them. These robots work continually, day and night, going where no robot has gone before, tirelessly updating their masters' indexes. It's quite important to understand the basic principles of the way they work.

First of all the robot goes to the home page of a web site that the search engine knows about. It might have already indexed the site and wants to update its index, or it might be a newly listed site that it is going to index for the first time. It indexes this page.

The robot then follows links from that page and indexes the pages that the links lead it to. Remember this point as it is important to keep in mind when you are designing your pages (more on this in Step Four.) These might be additional pages on the same web site, or they might be links to pages on other sites. In this way it crawls all over the Internet, indexing more and more pages as it goes about its busy job. In addition to indexing the actual pages on a site, it also gathers other facts and figures such as which sites link to and from which other sites.

Some people are fearful that robots can cause problems, such as spreading viruses. Web-indexing robots do not do anything harmful. However, you may very well want to restrict the pages that get indexed; perhaps you have sensitive information on your site that you don't want the whole world to know about, such as information intended for your employees or customers only. Or you may want to restrict a robot from a particular search engine from indexing certain pages.

This is why you need to have a robots.txt file.

The robots.txt file is simply a text file that sits in the root directory of your web site. It may contain instructions for robots, or it may be completely empty. Even if you are quite happy for all robots to index all pages on your site, it's still a good idea to have an empty robots.txt file on your site, as most robots will look for this file first. But nothing drastic will happen if you don't have one.

The robots.txt file contents

The instructions you're most likely to want in your robots.txt file are details of which directories or pages you **don't** want the robots to visit.

Consider the following two lines:

```
User-agent: *
Disallow: /
```

"User-agent" means "robot or spider name". Each search engine's robot has a specific name (you can find a list of them on the Web Robots Page at www.robotstxt.org/wc/robots.html).

In the example shown here, the * is a wildcard character which means ALL ROBOTS.

"Disallow" refers to the directories that you do not want the robots to visit. In the example shown, the single / character indicates all directories on the site are off-limits.

Here are a few additional examples:

```
User-agent: *
Disallow: /company/employees
```

This means that all robots should not index anything in the employees directory.

```
User-agent: googlebot
Disallow: /yahoo
```

This tells the Google robot not to index anything in the yahoo directory.

Important Note!

Compliance with the instructions in the robots.txt file is entirely voluntary, and there are no guarantees that all robots that visit your site will do as you ask. So if you have truly sensitive information on your site, you must find other ways of securing it.

Get more info

For more information about robots and how to modify your robots.txt file, see the Web Robots Page at www.robotstxt.org/wc/robots.html.

Step Two: Get Indexed

The next step is to make sure that all the important search engines know about your web site (in other words, they have indexed it). You can easily check this.

Go to the search engine's home page - e.g. www.google.com.

In the search field, enter the word "site:" followed by your web site address — for example, site:www.mysite.com — and click on the Search button.

It will shortly come back with a list of all pages that it has indexed on your site. If the list is empty, now would be a good time to submit it. Each search engine has its own guidelines for submitting sites. Following is a list of some of the popular search engines' site submission pages:

google.com: http://www.google.com/addurl/
google.co.uk: http://www.google.co.uk/addurl/
Yahoo Shopping: http://add.yahoo.com/fast/help/us/shop/cgi_crawl
MSN: http://search.msn.com/docs/submit.aspx?

NOTE: We can't guarantee the continued accuracy of these links. If they do not work, go to the search engine's home page and look for instructions on adding a site. Many search engines (such as AOL for example) use the Google engine these days, so Google should definitely be your first port of call!

Asking to have your site indexed by a search engine does not guarantee that it will be. They each have their own criteria for deciding whether to index a site or not. If you have previously submitted your site and it has not been indexed, you should follow the instructions in the rest of this book, paying particular attention to the following:

- Make sure that all of the pages on your site contain meaningful, relevant information. If you have "spam" pages (pages that contain nothing but lots of keywords and keyphrases and little else), your site is likely to be blacklisted.
- Make sure that there are links TO your site from other VALID sites. What's a valid site? Basically, a web site that contains useful information and is not a "link farm". Link farms are simply pages and pages of links to web sites that have been set up in the mistaken belief that the more links you have to your site, the better for search engine rankings. Whilst this is true in theory, most search engines will not only ignore these meaningless links but they may actually penalise you for using them. So avoid them like the plague!
- Make sure that all the pages on your site are linked together (see Step Five for more details)

Once your site is indexed by a search engine, you DO NOT need to keep resubmitting it. It will remain indexed unless it is removed for some specific reason — for example, if somebody complains about the content of your site, or if it is "out of action" and unreachable.

What about those search engine submission services and programs?

It might be useful to use one of these services ONCE, when you are getting started, but after that they are pointless and, in fact, some search engines will penalise you for continually bombarding them with indexing requests. And most of them will ignore automated submissions anyway. So our advice is not to waste your time or money on such services. You would do much better to manually submit your site to the search engines that matter.

Speaking of which ...

Which search engines matter?

At the time of writing, and in my personal experience, the most significant search engines are, roughly in order of importance:

Google
MSN
Yahoo
AOL
Lycos
Ask Jeeves

There may also be important search engines specific to your industry, and you should research those and add them to your list. As an example, for software publishers:

versiontracker.com
tucows.com

Step Three: Keywords are the Key

When you are searching for something on a search engine, you type in some words that relate to the product or service you're after. These are called keywords. When search engines are indexing your site, they pick out keywords from each page and add them to their index database. Keywords are given rankings depending upon various factors, such as:

- Their "density" within the page (how often each keyword appears)
- Their inclusion in the page title
- Their inclusion in the page's meta tags (in particular, the "keywords" meta tag, surprise, surprise!)
- Their relevance to the page content
- Their inclusion as part of the document name

There are other factors, which change from time to time and from search engine to search engine, but those are the basics that you need to keep in mind.

Keywords and Keyphrases

Keywords are individual words.

Keyphrases are groups of words that give a more specific meaning than a single word. They don't need to make sense. For example, if your site specialises in selling books in braille, "books" is a keyword but it isn't a very useful one because it is such a common word; "books braille" is much more meaningful from a search engine's point of view.

Noisewords

Noisewords are those small words that appear everywhere and have no relevance as far as searching is concerned. For example: ***and***, ***the***, ***or***, ***it***, and so on. You can ignore such words when building your list of keyphrases.

Now would be a good time to do the following exercise:

Think carefully about what keywords people would use to find your product or service. Make a list of those words or phrases. Be creative! Put yourself in your potential customers' shoes and try to imagine how they would go about looking for your web site.

Let's look at some examples.

Suppose your web site sells car parts. That's a very wide scope! The obvious keyphrase would be "car parts". But that is a very competitive keyphrase – there will be thousands and thousands of matches and your chances of coming out on top are very slim, no matter how good your web site is.

So put yourself into a buyer's shoes. You probably know what make of car you need the part for and you would be likely to include that in your search. For example, you might search for "car parts for a volkswagen golf". If your site sells Volkswagen parts, then, one of your keyphrases should be "car parts volkswagen golf" (remember what I said about the noisewords!).

Mis-spellings

Here's an idea to make your list of keyphrases grow even more :)

Lots of people are not very good at spelling. To improve your chances even more, you should allow for these.

Looking at our car parts example again, how do you spell "Volkswagen"? Volksvagen? Volkswagon? Volkswaggon?

How about a certain popular page layout program? Is it "QuarkXPress"? "Quark Xpress"? "Quark Express"? "QuarkExpress"? Or simply "Quark"?

Alternative Spellings

Not exactly the same as mis-spellings, these are valid alternative ways of spelling a word. Quite a few words are spelled differently in UK English than US English. Here are a few examples:

catalogue (UK spelling)
catalog (US spelling)

check (US spelling)
cheque (UK spelling)

licence
license
(both valid)

If any such alternatives apply to whatever you are promoting on your website (or should that be "web site"?), you should know what they are, and consider adding them to your keyphrases.

Synonyms

Synonyms are words that have a similar meaning. You might use a thesaurus to look up synonyms for a word (some word processors, such as Microsoft Word, have a built-in thesaurus). There's a useful online resource for finding synonyms at www.synonym.com/synonym. See if you can think of any appropriate synonyms for each word in each keyphrase. For example, the word "car" has the following synonyms:

auto, *automobile*, *motorcar*, *vehicle*.

Plurals

Theoretically, search engines should find pluralised versions of keywords. However in practice I've found that this is not always reliable. So my advice is to **include the pluralised versions** of your keywords. A search on "books about grammar" will find somewhat different results to a search on "book about grammar".

Extended words

Most search engines will find meaningful partial word matches. By "meaningful" I mean that if you search for "native" it won't match words like "alternative". On the other hand, if you search for "publish" it might well match "publishing". Whilst it will not do any harm to include both versions, if you find that your keyphrase list is getting a bit out of hand, you can pare it down by removing the shorter versions of such words. But first run a quick check by doing a search in a few search engines using your keywords.

Location

If the business you're promoting is specific to a particular area, it's important to include the location in all your keyphrases. Restaurants are a good example: if you're looking for an Indian restaurant you would probably prefer to find one in your local area. So you would search for something like "indian restaurant birmingham".

Complete your keyphrase list

Add all the mis-spelling, alternative spelling, synonym and plural options you can think of to each keyphrase. You may end up with keyphrases that look like this:

car auto vehicle parts spares volkswagen volksvagen volkswagon volkswaggon

car auto vehicle parts spares cadilac cadillac caddy

catalog catalogue publishing quarkxpress quark xpress express quarkexpress

There are several free tools available on the internet to help you figure out your keywords. One of them is the Keyword Selector Tool provided by Overture at http://inventory.overture.com/d/searchinventory/suggestion/

The page is quite simple:

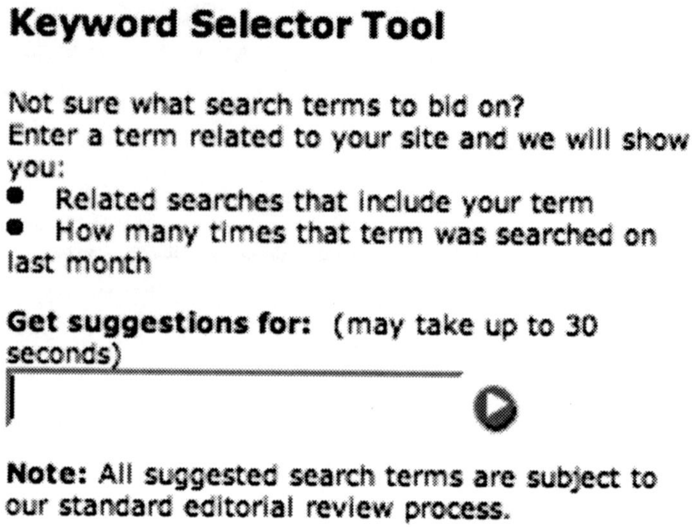

Enter a keyword or phrase into the search box and click the arrow. You'll be rewarded with a list showing the popularity of your keyword, and some suggestions for similar keywords and phrases. For example, when I searched on "seo" I got the following very enlightening result:

Count	Search Term
53811	seo
8996	seo services
8719	seo company
6754	dw230 seo
6427	seo tool
6404	blog seo unofficial
5234	seo expert
4820	internet marketing seo
4627	seo firm
4452	search engine optimization seo
4127	seo optimization
3906	seo copywriting
3495	seo training
3298	seo software
3192	engine promotion search seo software strategy
2942	seo web design
2700	seo consultant
2297	seo blog
2190	seo service
2043	seo consulting
1941	seo marketing
1829	seo taiji
1765	affordable seo
1592	learn seo
1589	seo book
1568	seo tip

(There's a lot more, which you can't see in this screen shot.) The Count column shows the number of searches that were done on that keyword during the preceding month.

From this result I created the following keyphrase list:

seo
seo services
seo company
seo tool
seo expert
linternet marketing seo
seo firm
search engine optimization seo
seo optimization
seo training
engine promotion search seo seo
web design
seo consultant
seo service
seo consulting
seo marketing
affordable seo
learn seo
seo book
seo tip
seo article
seo workshop
seo class
web site seo
seo specialist
professional seo
seo news
seo course
seo web site design
seo strategy
seo ranking
seo solution
seo ebook
affordable seo services
seo promotion
seo courses
seo training course
seo help
seo consultancy
affordable business seo small
budget seo
basics learn seo

Some of these results are quite interesting. I would never have thought of including "seo firm" but it's up there near the top of the popularity chart. And note that you can click on one of the phrases in the list to conduct a search based on that phrase. Looking over this list, it's clear that there is some duplication: "seo", for example, is included in most of the keyphrases, so there's no need to have it on its own. Similarly, we've got both "seo services" and "affordable seo services" – we can do away with the first one since it's included in the second one. In this way I reduced my list to this:

affordable budget seo service services
seo company firm
seo tool
seo expert
Internet marketing seo
search engine optimization optimisation seo
seo training class course courses learn
search engine promotion seo
seo consultant consultancy marketing
learn basics seo
seo book ebook
seo tip tips
seo workshop
seo specialist
professional seo
seo news
seo web site design
seo strategy
seo solution
seo promotion
seo help
affordable budget business seo small

Notice the inclusion of the synonyms “budget” and “affordable”, and “company” and “firm”. Also note the inclusion of the alternative spellings “optimization” (US spelling) and “optimisation” (UK spelling).

So that’s a pretty good result for “seo”. But what other keywords and phrases should we consider? Not everybody is familiar with the term “seo”, so what might such people search for? How about “search engine ranking”? A search on that phrase in the Overture tool provided me with lots more useful ideas for keyphrases.

Here’s an idea for another good way to find effective keywords: see what the competition is doing! Go to Google and do a search on your most important keyphrase and see who comes up top of the results (ignoring any paid ads). Click on the link and then look at their keywords. To do this, select the “View Source” or “Page Source” option in your web browser and look for the keywords meta tag. Using my previous “volkswagen spare parts” example, these are the keywords from the top-placed result page:

<meta name=”keywords” content=”Vw parts,vw spares,volkswagen wheels,volkswagen parts and salvage,golf parts,vw,vw parts,volkswagen golf parts,volkswagen parts,parts,volkswagen polo,used golf spares,used golf

parts,passat spares,passat parts,vento,bora,corrado,audi,skoda,seat,cheap spares,panels,sharan,vento,gti,gti parts,cabrio,engine,gearbox,vw salvage, parts,sciroccos,jetta,transporter,german cars,parts,used passat spares,used passat parts, used polo parts, used polo spares,Golf,Parts,catalytic converter,power steering rack,radiators,condenssor,compressor,throttle body volkswagon parts" />

This immediately brings to light a few that I hadn't thought of:

vw, salvage, german cars, catalytic converter, etc.

Ask your colleagues and your customers for their suggestions as well – they will probably come up with some good ideas that you hadn't thought of.

You should also regularly review your web site's logs. Most hosting companies provide a log analysis program - popular ones include Webalizer and Analog. These programs analyze the activity logs that are almost certainly maintained on your web site, and provide all kinds of fascinating information such as how many people have visited your site, which pages they looked at, which countries they were from, what time of day is most active, what sites referred them to yours via links, and – most importantly for our purposes – what keywords they used to find your site.

I know what you're thinking: "But I could end up with a list of **dozens** of keyphrases!"

So what?

List them in order of popularity (as determined using the Overture tool described above), making sure that you include only phrases that are truly relevant to your site.

Competitive Keywords

The more people are likely to use a particular keyword or phrase, the more competitive it is. In other words, the harder it will be to get a high placement in the search results on that word or phrase. "SEO", for example, is an extremely competitive keyword. This is why it's so important to include as many of the less competitive keyphrases as you can. In the next step you'll see how these are put to use.

When you've made your keyphrase list you are ready to proceed to Step Four.

Step Four: Create Pages

Memorise this phrase:

CONTENT IS KING!

There was a time, way back in the dim distant history of the Internet, when you could create a web page with some pictures and a bit of text, then add a whole bunch of keywords to your meta tags, and the search engines would index the page using those keywords.

Not any more!

The search engine indexers are much more canny these days. They may consider your meta tag keywords, but – more importantly – they will look at the words that appear in the page.

In order for your web pages to be indexed and receive good rankings, they must contain RELEVANT CONTENT.

And that content must be in a form that the search engine robots can digest. This means that it must be in actual text within the HTML. It cannot be embedded within a Flash movie or some other graphic format, because the robot cannot extract the text from it. If you already have a beautifully designed web site that consists of several pages of Flash movies, and you are wondering why your site can't be found on Google, this explains why. But don't despair – you don't need to scrap your site and re-create it in boring old HTML. You can create additional pages, as described in this chapter, and link them to your Flash pages (and vice versa).

Remember that list of keyphrases you made? Your next step is to create a page for **each keyphrase**.

Each page will be highly targeted to people searching for specific things. We will call these our **Reference Pages**.

Each page should follow a certain set of rules.

The Reference Page Rules

1. Each page is devoted to one specific topic (i.e., one specific keyphrase)

2. The text must be presented in well-formed HTML: no mis-matched tags! You can find a free HTML validity checker here:

   http://validator.w3.org/

3. The page must contain at least four paragraphs of meaningful, relevant information about its topic. This must be readable, well-written text with no typos or grammatical errors. If it's poorly written, boring, or not relevant to the keyphrase, all your efforts will have been wasted because you'll lose them before they've had a chance to get to your main page. You might like to get a copy of my grammar reference book, ***The Grammar Cookbook***, which provides easy-to-understand descriptions of the most common grammatical errors, and how to fix them. See www.trackerpress.com.

4. All of the words in your keyphrase must be used within the page's text at least twice (yes, even the mis-spellings). The more they are used, the better! (Without being silly.) Use them in proper, meaningful sentences. Now I realise that my comment about including the mis-spellings contradicts what I just said about typos and grammar. You'll need to be a bit creative here. First, only include the most common mis-spellings – there shouldn't be more than two or three, generally. Then you can insert some witty comment such as "You might call it a Volkswaggon, but to us they're all Volkswagens!" If you can't think of a good way to slip them in, then leave them out. Some search engines (Google, for example) will alert you if they think you've made a spelling mistake anyway – so test yours to see what you get when you enter them into Google.

5. The page title must be relevant and should contain the main keywords.

6. The Description meta tag should contain a brief, accurate description of the page, using the main keywords for that page. This is very important because it is what will probably be displayed in the search engine's result page. (See the discussion of meta tags at the end of this list.)

7. All the words in the page's keyphrase should be included in the keywords meta tag. Simply list them, in lowercase, with a comma in between each keyword or phrase, like this:

   word,a phrase,another phrase,stuff,more stuff,plural stuff

8. Include links to other pages on your site – at an absolute minimum, to your home page or to the product or service's main page. The best way is to have a navigation bar or set of buttons or links in your page template.

9. The page must have a pleasing appearance. This is going to be the point of entry to your web site for many people, and you know what they say about first impressions! You don't want to scare them off right away with an ugly page. The best way is to create a template and modify the content for each individual page. Don't forget to also modify the page title, description, and keywords tags!

10. Give the page a meaningful name. Most search engines index page names as well as their content. Use underscores or hyphens to separate words – here are a few examples:

    car-parts-volkswagen.html

    wedding-dresses.html

    phone-accessories.html

    yoga-instruction-classes.html

    indian-restaurant-glasgow.html

    I'm sure you get the picture!

Remember what I said about competitive keyphrases in Step Three? It's most important to create reference pages based on some of the less-competitive keyphrases in your list. If we look back at my list of "SEO" keywords from the Overture Keyword Selector Tool, the most popular keyword is, not surprisingly, "SEO", with over 53,000 searches being done on that keyword in one month. This means that everybody with an SEO-related site will want to include that keyword and there will be many thousands of results for a search on it. The chances of coming near the top of that search are pretty slim!

Further down the list we find "seo tip" with 1568 votes and – even further down – "development seo web" with 701. As long as they are actually relevant to your site, you should include lots of those lower-ranking keyphrases.

"But what's the point?" you may well ask, "if only 700 people use that search term, as compared to over 53,000 for the top one?"

Well, think of it this way: Is it better to come near the top of a number of less-popular searches, or totally lost in thousands and thousands of results for the most popular ones? It's like joining a lottery syndicate: you have a far better chance of winning something, although your winnings will be smaller. But would you rather have a share of **something**, or all of **nothing**?

Meta Tags

Meta tags are information inserted into the "head" area of a web page. Some people argue that meta tags are dead, because search engines no longer use them to index pages. While it is true that the **keywords** meta tag is far less important than it was just a few short years ago, I feel that it is still worth including. These are the tags you need to include in your pages:

title – This tag is essential as it determines the title of the page as it will appear in the web browser's window title. It will also be indexed and used during searches.

description – Many search engines will display the description meta tag with the search results. If you don't include a description tag, it will pick text more or less at random from the page. This tag will also be indexed.

keywords – well you know all about those now, don't you?

Here's an example of a good set of meta tags:

```
<head>
<title>CatBase - The Database Publishing So-
lution</title>

<meta name="description" content="Cross media
database publishing solutions for publishing
a catalog, directory, price list, or any da-
tabase-based data.">

<meta name="keywords" content="indesign,frame
maker,XML, association, directories, automat-
ed, catalog, publishing, software, Catalogue,
CatBase, classified ads, data, database, data-
base publishing, directories, directory, pub-
lish, Pagination, personnel, Quark, express,
xpress, Quarkxpress,Quark Xpress, cross me-
dia, cross-media">
</head>
```

I've added the line spacing just for clarity.

(There will probably be additional tags within the <head> section.)

What Not To Do

1. Do not create pages that are stuffed with a disproportionately high use of keywords or loads of keywords simply strung together in nonsensical

sentences. Be sensible and use the keywords in meaningful sentences.

2. Do not create pages that are simply lists of links to other pages on your site or to other websites, with the exception of your site map and/or reference index page (see Step Five).

3. Do not stuff your pages with irrelevant popular keywords. You can get lists of the most popular current keywords and – in theory – add them to your pages to increase your hit rate. I **do not** recommend doing this! You'll probably get away with something like "Britney Spears likes this kind of food" but don't push your luck: somebody might complain to Google, MSN, etc. and they may very well remove your site from their index altogether.

4. Don't use hidden tags or links to hide illicit keywords – they will probably be ignored and you may even be penalized for them.

Update Your Pages

Once you've created your reference pages and uploaded them to your web site, you can forget about them for a while. But not for too long! It's a good idea to update your pages once in a while – especially your home page. Some people feel that this will encourage the robots to reindex your pages more frequently. I'm not entirely convinced of this, but what harm can it do? And the fact is that if you go back and revisit your pages a week or two after creating them, you'll see errors that you didn't see before, or think of a better way to describe something or some additional information or new keyphrases that you can create pages for.

If you've ended up with a long list of keyphrases, the idea of creating a reference page for each one might seem a bit daunting. But you don't have to do them all at once! Prioritise your list and just start with the top few. You can then add more pages when you have the time – maybe you could set a goal of adding two new pages a week, or something like that.

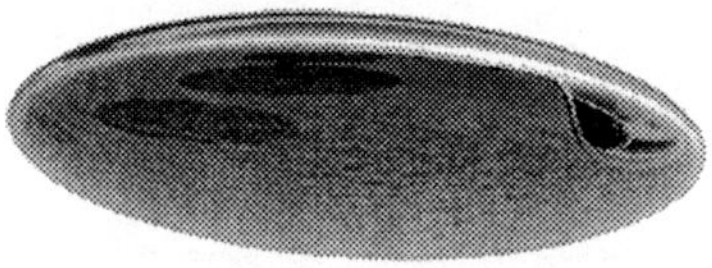

Step Five: Link ’em up

This is the final step, and it’s a very important one!

As explained earlier, search engine robots work in the following way:

1. They start at your home page, or at a page on your site that another site has linked to

2. From there they follow links to other pages

So it is most important that you **link your pages up**! There are several ways to do this – all of them important.

Links from your home page

You MUST have links from your home page to your reference pages and to your site map, and these links must be plain text links, not embedded in Javascipt menus and the like.

If you have a beautiful Javascript menu and you don’t want to spoil the look of your home page, you can just add a row of links at the very bottom of the page, and set them in a small font size and in a colour that won’t stand out too much. Or create a site map and simply have a link to that from the home page.

Don’t put these links within a “hidden” tag, as search engines may choose to ignore them.

You don‘t need to create a link to **each** reference page from your home page. As long as the robot can follow links and eventually reach all your pages in that way, that’s what is important. So you could have an index page listing all your reference pages, and have a link to that page from your home page.

As an example, take a look at the CatBase_web site at www.catbase.com. You'll notice a link to **Tutorials** on the home page, which links to an index page listing all the tutorial pages. The Tutorial pages are the site's reference pages: each Tutorial page covers one specific aspect of the program – for example, "Publishing a Catalogue with QuarkXPress".

Add a Site Map

A site map is a page that shows a hierarchical representation of the pages on your website, with links to those pages. It's useful for people to find something specific, and it's also useful for robots to build their page indexes. Have a link to the site map from every page, ESPECIALLY your home page.

The following example is a portion of the site map from the CNN site:

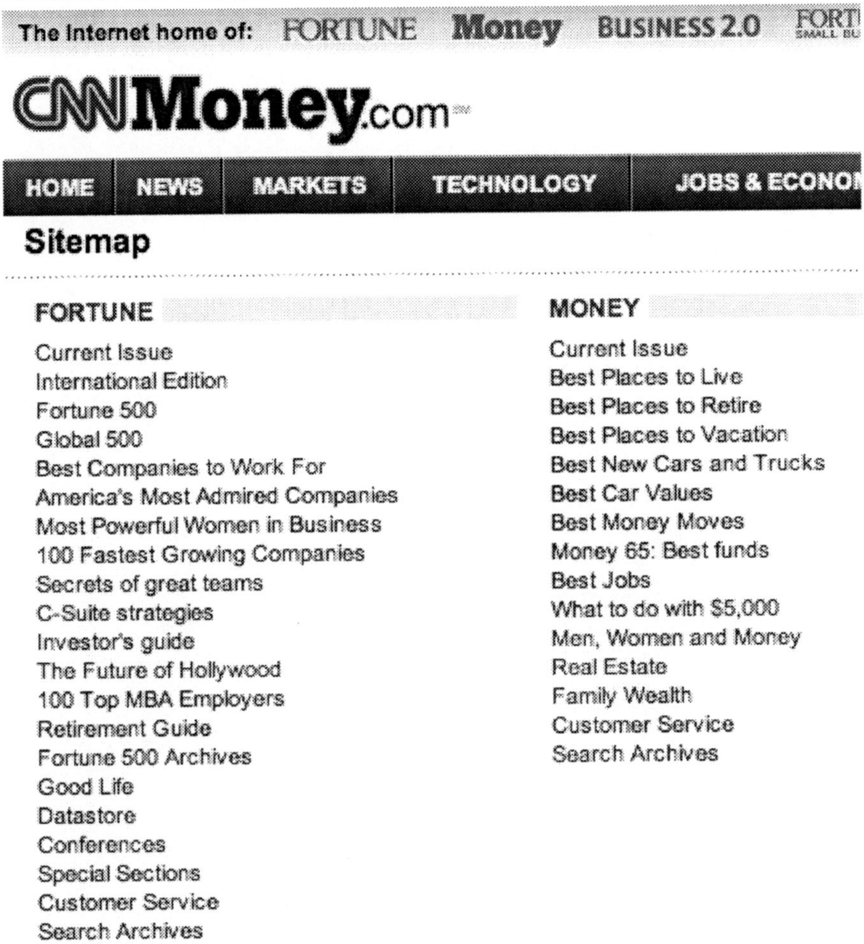

Get Other Sites to Link to Yours

When calculating a website's page ranking, search engines will take into consideration how many, and what quality of, other sites link to it. You'll get bonus points if there are links to your site from a well-respected site, and demerits if there are links from disreputable sources such as link farms (link farms are simply pages and pages of links to other web sites, with no relevance to anything).

You may need to do a bit of research for this. Look for websites that offer information relevant to your industry: user groups, business directories (local business directories are very good), and special interest sites, for example.

It can be useful to "exchange links" with other websites offering something similar or complementary to yours. For example, if you're a florist, you might contact businesses in your local area such as funeral parlours and wedding planners and offer to include a little blurb and a link to their site in exchange for them doing likewise for you. Just make sure that they are reputable and relevant. In this way you bag two fish with one hook: you add to your linked-from count and – who knows – you might even get some new business from them.

Who's Linking to Your Site?

You can get a good idea of what pages link to your site by checking which ones have been indexed by various search engines. To do this, go to the search engine's home page (google.com, for example) and type into the query field:

link:www.yoursitename.com

You might find all kinds of interesting links! You may be surprised to see which sites have linked to yours.

Note that this will not necessarily give you a list of all sites that link to yours – just the ones that the search engine has indexed. In fact in my experience, these lists are far from accurate.

Be sure to check all the main search engines.

You can find additional information about who's linked to your site by looking at your logs using a log analyser (see Appendix I).

But does it really work?

You bet!

If you want proof that this five-step method works, go to Google and search on “publish catalog quark” and see how close the “Publish a catalogue with QuarkXPress” page from the CatBase website comes to the top of the list! As this book was being written, it appeared in the No. 3 position on the first page of about 757,000 results – see the following screen shot:

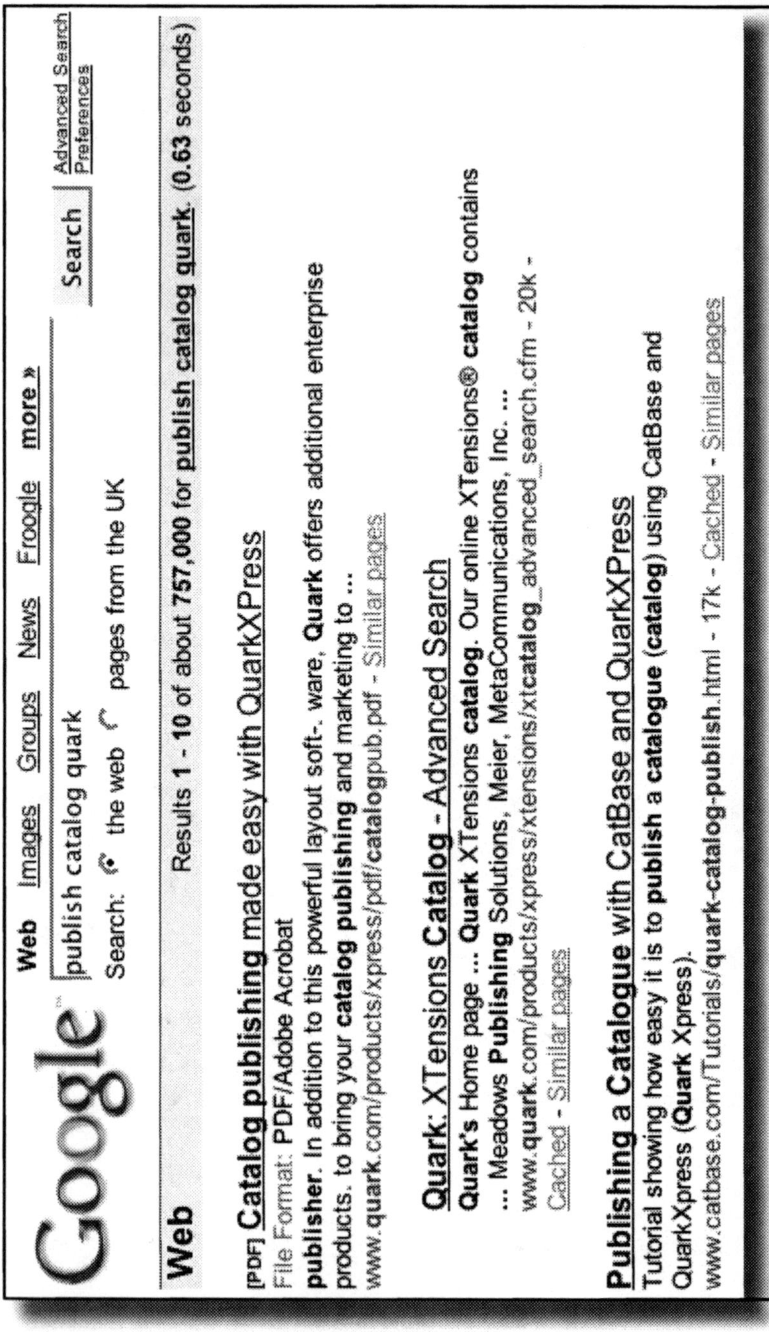

Notice the words that Google has highlighted: **Publishing** and **Catalogue** in the page title

publish, **catalogue**, **catalog**, and **Quark** in the page description.

quark, **catalog**, and **publish** in the page name

These are words that Google has indexed. You can probably figure out what the keyphrase for this page is:

publish catalog catalogue quark xpress quarkxpress

What next?

Now it's time for you to get to work! Just follow the five simple steps described in this book and you'll be amazed at the results you achieve.

In the Appendix you'll find a few additional suggestions to help you improve your web site's search engine rankings.

And don't forget to let me know how you get on! I'm always happy to hear from you – just email your comments, questions, and suggestions to pat@trackerpress.com.

Appendix I: More Suggestions

Web Site Logs

Most web sites (certainly ones that are commercially hosted) create log files. These files contain detailed information about who has visited your site – pages and pages of it! But using a log file analyzer, you can get very useful info from these files. Most hosting companies provide a log analysis program; popular ones include Analog and Webalizer. If you're not sure, check with your hosting company.

You should check your log files regularly. They will tell you such things as:

- How many people have visited your web site
- Which pages they looked at
- What files they downloaded
- How they got there: which other site referred them (via a link), or what search phrases they used
- Graphs that show which days were the busiest, and which hours of the day tend to be the busiest

PDF Documents

It might surprise you to learn that the contents of PDF documents on web sites get indexed, too. So if you have PDFs relating to your product or service, it's worth putting them on your web site.

A good example of how this idea can be fruitful is with books. You can extract individual pages from the PDF document and offer them as sample pages, as we have done with other Tracker Press titles (see http://www.trackerpress.com/sample-pages/samples.php

Pages can be extracted from PDF documents using Adobe Acrobat Professional. Don't forget that document names will be indexed! Give each PDF document that you create a meaningful name; instead of calling it "Page_25.pdf" give it a name that contains the main keywords from the document.

Make sure that there is a link to your web site on each PDF document! When somebody clicks on the link to a PDF document, it will be downloaded to their computer and then opened, or opened directly within the web browser, without visiting one of your web pages at all. So you must make sure that each document identifies you and provides a link back to your site.

PDF documents are indexed by many search engines besides Google! Wikipedia, for example, includes links to quality documents in its reference entries.

Appendix II: Useful Resources

Please note that these resources are accurate at the time of going to press, but we can't be sure that they will remain!

Finding Keywords

Overture:
http://inventory.overture.com/d/searchinventory/suggestion/

Google Adword Keywords Keyword Tool:
https://adwords.google.com/select/KeywordToolExternal

Checking Links

It's a good idea to check the links on your pages regularly: the internet is constantly changing and evolving, as your own web site should be, and links can easily become out-dated. Here is a free tool that will check all the links on a specified page and tell you if any of them are bad:
http://www.anybrowser.com/cgi-bin/checklinks.pl

Checking your Site's Indexing Status on Google

Google provides a useful tool for you to find out information about how and when it has indexed your web site:
https://www.google.com/webmasters/tools/siteoverview

Index

Let us keep in touch with you!

From time to time we send out an e-newsletter containing tips, updates, and suggestions to help you continue to improve your SEO skills. If you would like to receive the newsletter, please send an email to

fivesteps@trackerpress.com

with "newsletter" in the subject line.

You can also use this address to send us your own success stories and tips. We love to hear from our readers, so don't be shy! We promise to read every email we receive, and to respond if appropriate.

www.trackerpress.com

Tracker Press

Other Books from Tracker Press

The Grammar Cookbook

by Pat Bensky

The pages that you create for your web site should be not only relevant but READABLE as well! And in order for them to be readable and credible, they **must** be grammatically correct.

The Grammar Cookbook is an easy-to-read reference to the most common grammatical errors, which no business person or webmaster should be without. It provides quick, easy-to-find answers to such questions as

Is it "its" or "it's"?
Which is correct - "i.e." or "e.g."?
"ensure" or "insure"?
"stationery" or "stationary"?

The information is presented in a clear, easily understood topic-per-page format, with examples and amusing anecdotes to keep it light.

See www.trackerpress.com for more details!

Living Among Angels

by David Zimmer and Luella Stroh

Although many people believe in angels, they probably don't realize that thousands of angels live among mankind throughout the world just as Jesus, Abraham, and Buddha did. Similarly, the majority of mankind is unaware of how they are influenced by these angels. Those known as Lafayette, Nostradamus, Joan of Arc, and John Quincy Adams were a few of the angels who have lived among us. These angels, as well as those who were less well-known, profoundly impacted the lives of millions of people because they were vibrant role models.

Living Among Angels reveals the process that every spirit goes through to become an angel, and why we aren't aware of angels living among us.

See www.trackerpress.com for more details!

If you would like to be added to our mailing list, please send an email to mailinglist@trackerpress.com

Printed in the United Kingdom
by Lightning Source UK Ltd.
127165UK00001B/97/A

9 780954 610531